Adventurous And Interesting

Stories For Your Kids

*Mind-Blowing True Tales Guarantee That
Your Kid Will Fall In Love With Reading*

D1557183

Mattie Gardner

Contents

Introduction

Hi, My dear small and big reader! Do you want to impress your buddies at school? Do you need to think of something fun to do at Thanksgiving or Christmas? Do you want to learn a bunch of random facts about history, science, animals and the paranormal?

This is the perfect book for you! Thank you choosing this book!

Before we explore this book, let me introduce myself. My name is Mattie Gardner. I am a children book author, a storyteller and a teacher. I have been writing children book for more than 10 years and had published 6 books. Most of them are the series of Interesting Stories for Curious Kids. I have my own YouTube channel. I share stories twice a week on my channel with the kids all over the world.

OK, Are you ready to explore some epic, mind-blowing true stories and adventures with me? I can guarantee that you never heard or saw the stories and adventures in your life.Not from any TV or movies! Ready for the

adventure? Get your seat belt on! Let's go!

In this book you will find out a lot of fantastic and amazing true stories. They included inspiring stories which happened in real person, what problem they're facing in their life, how they come up with brilliant and creative solution to solve the problem, how resilient human being can be in a tough situation, how to be a better, loving, caring human being, how to have a curious, creative and growing mindset in order to deal with your situation, how creative and curious individual change the world and other's life, a lot of fun facts about animals, science, history and Paranormal.

Here are some spectacular and adventurous chapter you are about to read:The man jumps from the space. A man who ran a marathon on his balcony. Why do animals hibernate? Harry Wolhuter, the man survived from a lion attack. History of eating competitions. Why the Grate Wall of China was built.And more......

I hope you like and enjoy the stories! I have put a lot of heart to collecting information and writing this book. It was a great and fun experience for me. The past few

years the Covid 19 has changed the wold. Even though we can't go out and hand fun with friends but I still want you to enjoy the fun of reading at home! Enjoy reading with your parents and kids! Thank you so much for the support! Happy Reading!

The Duck Hatched by a Human

Since humans started living with animals, we have been hand-rearing abandoned or neglected animals. There are even trained people who make this their life's mission. When caring for young animals, especially those that hatch from eggs, many tools are needed. This includes an incubator. This allows eggs to get constant heat while developing into a hatchling. But what should you do if you do not have an incubator or even a proper heat lamp? Betsy Ross was about to discover the answer.

Betsy Ross, a mother of three, from Visalia, California, felt that the day was just too wonderful to pass up and took her children to the closest park to play pickleball. Unfortunately, the day was about to turn sad as they found a duck nest destroyed by someone. All but one egg was smashed, and even this one was slightly cracked. Her children begged her to save the egg. As the egg wasn't leaking, Betsy thought that she had a small chance of saving it. She took the egg and contacted her local wildlife center to see if they could take on the responsibility of hatching the egg. But yet again, the day

took another sad turn. They couldn't take the egg, but they were willing to take the hatchling if Betsy could hatch it. That in itself was a tall order as Betsy had no incubator to keep the egg warm. Then suddenly she had an idea! She would keep the egg close to her and warm by storing it in her bra.

The area created by her underclothes allowed the egg to get the moisture and heat it needed to continue its development. The only other thing she needed to do was to turn the egg a few times a day to ensure that it was heated on all sides. That is where the egg stayed, night and day for 35 days. There were times that Betsy couldn't look after the egg, and that was when her husband stepped in to be an adopted duck dad.

Finally, the big day arrived. Soft peeps were heard from within the shell, known as pipping. Soon the beak was trying to push through the eggshell. With the egg now hatching, it couldn't remain in Betsy's bra. She needed to step up her game in duck care.

Betsy knew that after the duckling started pipping, she had between 12 and 18 hours to get everything the duckling would need. She built a hatching box with

the humidity the duck egg needed and a heating lamp that provided extra warmth. There was no longer a need to turn the egg as the duckling tried to break its way through the shell. However, after a day with little to no progress, Betsy became worried and called the vet. According to the vet, there was a chance the egg membrane—between the duckling and the shell—was causing the duckling to become stuck. Betsy would have to slowly peel the shell away from the duckling to help it escape. Not doing this would cause the duckling to suffocate and die. But with a lot of patience and a little luck, she managed to free the duckling.

However, life had not been easy for this little duckling, and even after she got him out of his shell, he was still attached to the yolk, which was still attached to the egg. The duckling was a little premature and would need more time before he would be fully free from the egg.

After he was free, he was so weak. He didn't want to move or drink any water. Betsy was unwilling to lose her newly adopted feathered-child and took the time to help the duckling move and drink. Hour by hour he grew stronger until one day he was walking on his own. He even took to paddling around in puddles and in the

bathtub.

Despite Betsy being a rather odd-looking duck, the duckling thought she was his mother (called imprinting). He would happily follow Betsy wherever she went and would even cry if she left somewhere without him. They even decided to name him Thawn.

Sadly, the duckling could not stay with Betsy and her family as they didn't have a good enough home for him. Luckily, there was a rescue farm close by that willingly accepted Thawn. Here he could grow into a strong duck with a new human that loves him dearly. Do you think the other ducks ask him about his odd-looking mother?

The Man Who Ran a Marathon on His Balcony

In 2020, the world was devastated by the spread of the highly infectious COVID-19 virus. Countries around the world scrambled to control infections. Many places implemented lockdown procedures and encouraged no contact (social distancing) with other people. Unfortunately, this meant that many events were canceled. One of those events was the Barcelona Marathon. Many runners couldn't do anything but wait to see what would happen. However, one runner didn't sit back and wait. He laced up his shoes and ran that marathon, completing 26.2 miles on his 23-foot balcony.

Elisha Nochomovitz loved running marathons—having completed more than 30—and his personal best in completing one was 3 hours and 32 minutes. He was looking forward to the Barcelona Marathon, which was meant to be held on March 15, 2020. Once receiving word that the race would be canceled, he started making plans to run the race anyway. The thirty-two-year-old who lives in Balma, near Toulouse in southern France, was planning on completing the marathon as a virtual marathon.

The virtual marathon used the GPS in running watches—

or smartphones with apps such as Strava—to track the distance and time the runners achieved. However, as Elisha was in lockdown, he couldn't run in the streets, and not having a backyard left him with only one other choice. His 23-foot-long balcony.

First, he had to clean the balcony so he had the maximum length available to run on. Next, he had to calculate how many laps he would have to do. A 26.2-mile marathon is over 138,000 feet, and this meant that he would have to run over 6,000 laps. With the beautiful Pyrenees Mountain in the background, he couldn't think of a more beautiful place to run.

However, marathons aren't just physically challenging but are also mentally challenging. Elisa would be racing against the clock as there was no one else to run against. He would also be challenged by his mind constantly. This could possibly cause negative thoughts that he would have to overcome to complete the entire marathon without quitting.

On March 17, he started his run, listening to some of his favorite music to keep his energy levels up. The view also helped a little, and even his girlfriend was

there to ensure he had fresh shirts and water as he completed this challenge. Her cheers went a long way to help him succeed. These weren't the only things that were motivating him. He dedicated this race to all the medical professionals, who were risking their lives daily by treating those affected by COVID-19.

Everything was going well until he hit the 21-mile mark, and he was forced to stop and recharge his watch. However, once it was functioning again, he completed the marathon in a time of 6 hours and 48 minutes. Can you imagine how dizzy he would have been running back and forth for so many hours? However, some people didn't believe his amazing achievement. To prove them wrong, he ran a 30-mile marathon on the balcony again on March 24, 2020. That would have been over 6,800 laps.

Elisha was the inspiration many people needed to get some exercise despite the severe and often strict lockdowns. Many started to train in their backyard or simply run stairs to get their stiff muscles working again. He proved that you needed very little space to still remain in shape.

Man Jumps From Space

Humans have been fascinated with flight since they first saw birds flying. However, even with the invention of planes, people have tried to copy the feeling of flying by inventing many different extreme sports. If people aren't bungee jumping, they are parachuting from planes to get the heart-thumping experience of being weightless. However, one man took his love for free falling and combined it with his goal of breaking a world record. This resulted in the Red Bull Stratos $20 million project that claimed numerous world records and paved the way for science to learn more about space.

Felix Baumgartner was 16 years old when he enjoyed his first skydive. Before his feet even touched the ground, he knew that he would want more of this thrill. From then, he started BASE jumping with a parachute or wingsuit from cliffs and any other fixed structure he could find. He just loved being able to jump and fly through the air. He even approached Red Bull to sponsor him doing a BASE jump off the New River Gorge Bridge in West Virginia. They refused. However, they soon started to take notice of him as he continued to do

jump after jump. Then, about 32 jumps later, they were ready to sponsor him.

Yet, Felix still had one goal in the back of his mind: He wanted to break the world record of the highest freefall parachute jump. This record was held by Joseph Kittinger when he jumped from the Excelsior III at a height of 102,800 feet (approximately 19.4 miles). This record was set on August 16, 1960. Joseph was able to reach a maximum speed of almost 614 miles per hour and he fell for 4 minutes and 36 seconds. The record was held for 52 years by the time Felix performed his death-defying jump. It was a difficult task, but luckily for Felix, Joseph was still around and was willing to help the young man see his dream come true.

With the help of many, the preparation took many years and a lot of money. It wasn't just about the jump; it was about Felix's safety. He would have to be in a pressurized suit to allow for the jump that would beat the current record. Then, on October 14, 2012, in Roswell, New Mexico, they were ready.

Felix boarded a specially designed capsule, which would be transported to the stratosphere—the second layer

of the atmosphere—with a huge helium balloon. It took Felix about two hours to reach the height of 127,852 feet (about 24 miles). This is roughly 99,000 feet above Mount Everest. Once he was ready, the capsule was depressurized, and he was able to exit it with his new pressurized suit. He was able to sit on the edge of the capsule and admire the beautiful planet below him for a while as he mentally prepared himself for what he was about to do. Then, he jumped and started to free fall. It took him more than nine minutes to fall from the capsule until he was back on Earth. There were so many video cameras on him and on the capsule, the world sat with bated breath and watched his descent. You can still find many of these clips on the internet.

This amazing feat broke many records, including the first human to break the sound barrier while free falling, highest freefall parachute jump, fastest freefall (843.6 miles per hour), and the largest balloon used to get a human into space. However, it wasn't just about the jump and breaking records. There were advances in science that allowed scientists to test how a body handles extreme conditions in space. Not only that but they were also able to complete research about the

stratosphere, space in general, and improved safety equipment.

Felix has officially retired from being a daredevil and now works as a firefighter. However, to prove that science continues to progress, other people continue to keep breaking records. The highest freefall record was broken on October 24, 2014. Alan Eustace broke this record when he jumped from a height of 135,898 feet (almost 26 miles). Who knows what the future holds? Perhaps one day, free falling from space could become a tourist attraction.

Christiaan Barnard and the First Heart Transplant

In the past, when a person's organs started failing—either because of age, illness, or injury—there was no way to solve the problem and the person would die. As time progressed, organ transplants from human to human started to happen more often. However, some organ transplants just seemed impossible. One of these organs was the heart.

Transplanting a heart was considered a huge risk. Not only that, but finding a donor heart was difficult. Unlike kidneys and livers, a heart donation cannot come from a living donor and needs to be gifted after death. This changed on December 3, 1967 when a previously unknown doctor was about to be rocketed into stardom and medical history. This man was Christiaan Barnard, and thanks to him, a donor, his team of nurses, surgeons, and technicians, history was about to be made with the first human-to-human heart transplant.

Christiaan was born in Beaufort West in the Karoo, Western Cape, South Africa. As a young man, he studied to become a doctor and started showing interest in

cardiology when he delivered a baby with a heart defect. Unfortunately, as transplants weren't common at the time, the child died soon after. Christiaan felt that there must have been a way to have prevented this, to fix or replace damaged heart valves. During this time, the heart-lung machine was new, and no one dared to use it in their surgeries. This machine takes over for the heart's function when doctors operate on it, allowing for oxygenated blood (blood with oxygen in it) to still go through the whole body.

Christiaan was invited to Minneapolis and ended up working with Professor Wagensteen, where he could expand his medical knowledge. After spending a few years there, he returned to South Africa, but this time he had a gift with him. A now fully developed and working heart-lung machine. It was a wonderful gift from Professor Wagensteen that would soon play a vital role in opening the gateway to cardiac surgery.

In 1958, Christiaan returned to Groote Schuur Hospital, yet he wasn't ready to start with heart transplants just yet. He needed to start on something a little smaller. It was after his first successful kidney transplant on a woman called Edith Black that allowed him to lay the

groundwork and get the team members who would help him with the future heart transplant.

For a heart transplant to be successful—outside of the doctor and their team—there has to be a donor and a recipient. And not just any recipient, one who was willing to take the risk of going through the risky procedure. Louis Washkansky was one such man. He was in heart failure and didn't have long to live. He had nothing to lose and agreed to be experimented on if a heart could be found. Sadly (or luckily, depending on how you look at it), he didn't have to wait too long.

On Sunday, December 3, 1967, Denise Darvall, a bank clerk, was hit by a car. The accident killed her mother and left her so brain-damaged that the doctors felt she would never recover. When her father was approached about organ donation, he knew what he should do. His daughter was a kind spirit who loved to give things to people. The donation of her organs, including her heart, which went to Louis, would be her final gift to those who needed it. In death, she donated her heart and both her kidneys. Her name is cemented in the history books as the first human heart donor.

The operation to save Louis took nine hours and was deemed successful when the new heart started beating and he could wake up and speak to his family. However, Louis never left the hospital. He died 18 days later due to pneumonia caused by his weakened immune system. Up until his last breath, Denise's heart continued to be strong. Many cultures—past and present—view the heart as the soul of the person.

The operation was the first of many that paved the way to more difficult surgeries. Today, life-saving cardiac surgeries are available to not only adults but also children and babies, as long as there is a donor. The heart truly is connected to the soul as it is one life given to another.

Ring Around the Rosie – A Nursery Rhyme About the Black Plague

Ask anyone to sing Ring Around the Rosie and they will happily sing this to you:
Ring around the rosie,
Pockets full of posies;
Atishoo, atishoo (or ashes, ashes),
We all fall down.

Although the true history of this poem isn't known, many people think that it has a connection to the Black Plague. This disease nearly destroyed Europe and then again later London, England.

Fourteenth-century Europe—also known as the Middle Ages—wasn't the cleanest place in the world. Picture filthy streets covered in garbage and waste from chamber pots (early toilets). This filth was what caused the Black Plague. It attracted rats from every port because there was plenty of food they could eat lying in the street.

As if vermin underfoot weren't bad enough, they too carried their own vermin: fleas. These fleas weren't

alone though. They were infected with a bacteria called *Yersinia pestis*. The bacteria would block the mouths of the fleas as they tried to feed on the rats, causing the bacteria to be injected into the rats. This caused the rats to get the black plague. However, they didn't give the black plague to the humans. When the rats started to die of the disease, the fleas jumped onto anything else that they could feed on, and that was humans. With each bite, the fleas spread the disease to an unsuspecting population.

Depending on how the person was infected, resulted in different types of the plague: bubonic, pneumonic, and septicemic. The bites caused by the fleas resulted in the bubonic plague. People who had the bubonic plague would develop swelling in the lymph glands of their armpits and groins—known as buboes. As the disease worsened, the person developed more severe swelling. Some buboes were the size of apples! Later, small boils would cover most of their body. As the disease continued, the patient's skin would turn black, giving rise to the name Black Death.

Although the rats and fleas may have started the infection, they didn't spread it as far as was first

thought. The pneumonic plague was spread by the bacteria in the lungs being transmitted from human to human. This was done through droplets when the patient coughed or sneezed around uninfected people.

The septicemic plague was spread through the blood of an infected person. As bloodletting (intentional bleeding) was a popular way to treat ailments in the Middle Ages, this caused many people to come into contact with infected blood.

It is because of the spread of pneumonic and septicemic plague, that a third of Europe's population died. This was approximately 25 million people—within five years. In places such as Venice and Pisa—which lost three-quarters of their population—whole extended families were killed by the disease. There was no medicine to combat the disease, and no one knew how it was spreading. Boccaccio, an Italian writer, wrote that the disease was so bad that you would be eating lunch with your family and dinner with your ancestors in paradise.

This brings us back to the poem. In the first line, it talks about rosies. It is thought that this references the red rashes that formed as the disease was starting to take

hold.

In the second line, it mentions posies. There are two explanations for this. The first is that the people believed these posies (flowers) would protect them from the disease. Or second, the smell of the flowers would cover up the stinking dead bodies that still needed to be burned.

The third line could mean two things, depending on which version you know. Atishoo is the sound of a sneeze, which was one of the early symptoms of the disease which led to the pneumonic plague. In the version with ashes, this refers to the number of bodies that were burned, and the air was choked with the ash.

The last line simply means that everyone died. The untreated bubonic plague killed half of those infected. Meanwhile, the pneumonic and septicemic plagues killed all who were infected. The infected would die within 24 hours of getting the disease.

Scary, right? The scarier thing is that the plague never disappeared. The fleas would die during the winter, only for newly hatched fleas to reemerge during spring; the disease continued yearly but seemed to diminish

over time. However, another outbreak was seen in 1665 in England. This was known as the Great Plague, and it killed 100,000 Londoners, roughly 20% of the population.

Today, the bacteria causing the Black Plague can still be found in certain places in America, Africa, and Asia. It is found in host animals such as prairie dogs, rabbits, and squirrels, just to name a few. There are between 1,000 and 3,000 cases of Black Plague every year. Around 15 of these are found in the western United States. Once a person is infected, if they are not medicated within the first 24 hours, they will have the same survival rates as those in the Middle Ages. Thankfully, with antibiotics such as streptomycin, only 1–15% with the infection will be killed, instead of 100%. The Plague will always be around, and there is always a chance of someone getting infected and spreading it. This is why antibiotics are so important in destroying bacteria.

Real-Life Winnie-the-Pooh

Winnie-the-Pooh has been a part of children's lives for decades. This lively teddy bear was created by English author Alan Alexander Milne. His inspiration for the story was none other than his son Christopher Robin Milne and his collection of stuffed toys. Alan bought the teddy bear from Harrods in London, which became Winnie-the-Pooh for Christopher when he was just a year old. Soon his collection grew with a donkey (Eeyore), a piglet (Piglet), a kangaroo (Kanga), and lastly, a tiger (Tigger). These toys can still be found in the Polonsky Exhibition in the New York Public Library in Manhattan.

The first publication of Winnie-the-Pooh was in a newspaper in 1925, and the following year the first book was published. And though many people readily accept that a young boy and his toys were the inspiration for a much-loved bear, this isn't the complete truth. The truth is that Winnie-the-Pooh was based on a real bear donated to the London Zoo in 1914.

It all started in Canada. Harry Colebourn, a Canadian soldier and veterinarian, was just about to head

overseas to fight at the start of World War I. Thanks to his diaries, we know so much about what was about to unfold.

It was August 24, 1914 when he bought a black bear cub for $20. He named her Winnipeg Bear, after where he grew up. It wasn't long before she had a new nickname: Winnie. Even when Harry went to England, he took her with him on a ship. The little bear soon became a favorite of those who met her, and she even became the mascot for the 2nd Canadian Infantry Brigade. She did everything with them, but she had a special connection with Harry. She would play with him, allow him to feed her by hand, and cuddle when they had time to relax.

Sadly, word came that the 2nd Canadian Infantry Brigade would be traveling to France, and Winnie couldn't go with them. Heartbroken, Harry took her to the London Zoo on December 9, 1914, where they were only too happy to look after her until he could return. Even separated from Harry, she was still a loveable bear and soon became one of the most popular and beloved animals in the zoo. She was so tame young children could ride on her and adults could feed her by hand.

When Winnie was about 11 years old (1925), she came face-to-face with Christopher Robin. The little boy loved her so much that he ended up naming his teddy bear after her. The bear got its second name Pooh from a friend of Christopher's pet swan. And so, the name Winnie-the-Pooh was born. Winnie continued to live in the London Zoo until she died of old age on May 12, 1934, a much-loved and treasured animal.

You must be wondering what happened to Harry and why he never came back for her. Harry survived WWI, and when he returned, he saw just how much of an impact Winnie had on the lives of the people who met her. He couldn't take her away from her new home. He ended up donating her to the zoo so that she could continue to brighten the lives of those that came to see her.

Today, two statues of Harry and Winnie can be found in the London Zoo and in Winnipeg as a memorial to the two souls who brought joy to many people and continue to be the inspiration for a beloved teddy bear.

Why Do Salmon Swim Upstream?

Everyone knows that salmon swim upstream, but not everyone knows why. The easiest answer is that it is tradition. Their parents swam from the ocean to lay eggs in freshwater, and their grandparents did it, and their great-grandparents did it too. This migration is important for the survival of the salmon. Salmon are anadromous fish. This means they are born in freshwater but will migrate to saltwater after some time. Salmon spend most of their adult life in the ocean before returning to where they were born. This area is known as the spawning grounds.

How does the salmon do this? To understand how, you must first understand the lifecycle of salmon. There are five Pacific salmon (Chinook, pink, chum, sockeye, and coho) that migrate thousands of miles from the ocean to where they will lay their eggs. These salmon have to face many dangers in the ocean and freshwater. However, that isn't all. They use a lot of energy to swim and jump against the water (going upstream). While in freshwater, the salmon eat very little, if anything, so their energy continues to decrease. Some fish don't

even make it to the area where they will lay eggs (spawning ground), dying from exhaustion or being caught by predators such as bears.

It is believed that the fish know where to go by making a map from when they left the spawning grounds as a year-old fish (fry). As they travel toward the ocean, they memorize the route through the smells (scents) around them. If they manage to survive this journey, they will one day return to the spawning grounds. Other studies say these fish use the Earth's magnetic field to find their way back. Some fish get lost. However, they realize that the scent of the spawning ground isn't as strong, and then try to make their way back to where they should be.

Those that make it to the spawning ground, will lay and fertilize the eggs that will create new salmon. The female salmon digs a small hole in the riverbed with her tail. This is called a redd. She will then make about seven redds and fill each of them with about 2,500–7,000 eggs. Her job is now done, and the nearest male takes over. The male will fertilize the eggs with his sperm (milt) and then leave. Although salmon can live up to eight years, this trip uses so much energy,

the adults don't make their way back to the ocean. Instead, they end up dying within days of reaching the spawning ground. However, don't be too sad about this happening. Thanks to the salmon, many animals have food for the year. Even the fish that are partially eaten become fertilizer for the plants in the area.

Unfortunately, thanks to climate change and human involvement, it becomes more and more difficult for the salmon to reach their traditional spawning grounds. Although they can jump up waterfalls, they cannot jump over man-made dams. Thankfully, some people are helping these migratory fish complete their journey.

A salmon cannon, a large pipe system, allows salmon to travel long distances over dams and other difficult obstacles within seconds instead of taking hours. This cannon was invented by the people of Whooshh Innovations. The idea behind the invention is to allow safe passage for fish that make this difficult journey.

Not only that, but it prevents fish that are not supposed to be in the ecosystem from getting into them with a selective fish passage. This passage only allows certain fish to pass while stopping others from moving through.

Non-native fish (fish that are not supposed to be there) are destructive to habitats meant for native fish, and it is best to prevent them from being in those waterholes. The salmon cannon not only makes the trip faster but also lowers the number of injuries to the salmon as they swim upstream.

Although there aren't many of these cannons available everywhere, it is hoped that soon more will be made. This will allow many more salmon to reach the different spawning grounds easier and safer. This will help the environment by feeding many creatures in these areas.

Why Do Animals Hibernate?

When you think of winter, you think of the cold and snow. In some countries, people celebrate Christmas with lots of different and delicious foods. However, if you are a wild animal, there isn't that much food, if any. Animals that can't find food will leave the area (migrate) to places with more food, while others will hibernate. When animals hibernate, they seem to be asleep, but it isn't the same sleep you get when you tuck yourself into bed at night. Some animals seem to wake up from hibernation to get some slow-wave sleep. So, what is hibernation, and why do animals do it?

There are two types of animals: ectothermic and endothermic. Ectothermic animals need heat from the outside of their bodies, such as the sun, to warm them. These animals include reptiles (lizards, crocodiles, etc.), insects, and certain fish. Endothermic animals make their own heat and fuel it by eating. These animals are often called warm-blooded. Both types of animals seem to fall asleep during the colder months when there is little food for them. Ectothermic animals, such as insects, go through diapause, when there is a temporary

stop in development and the animal is unmoving. Endothermic animals go through hibernation to avoid freezing conditions when there is little to no food.

No food means endotherms don't have the fuel to keep themselves warm enough to survive winter. These animals enter an energy-saving mode called torpor. This causes them to have fewer bodily functions—their breathing slows, their heartbeat is slower, and their body temperature falls. This reduction in body functions allows them to conserve energy to get through difficult times. Hibernation is just a longer period of torpor, as it can last several hours or a whole season, depending on the animal. Animals such as the tawny frogmouth will go into daily torpor at night to reduce the amount of energy wasted while sleeping. This is especially true during winter as it will only be active during the day and unmoving at night.

Animals that hibernate for long periods will need to properly prepare or they will starve. During seasons with a lot of food, they need to consume as many energy-rich meals as possible. By eating so much, they can build up a store of body fat. An example of an animal that picks up extra pounds before winter is the

black bear. They can increase their weight by 29 pounds a week in preparation for hibernation. They do this by eating berries, fish, and any other food they find. The next step is to find a place to hibernate in safety. Bears will find a den, which they will line with leaves, twigs, and other materials to keep them warm as they sleep. Once hibernation starts, these animals will rarely wake for up to 100 days. They will not eat, drink, exercise, or even go to the bathroom. Bears are considered the largest of all the animals that hibernate.

Other animals, such as squirrels, can't migrate, and because of their small size, they lose more heat when it gets cold. And though they seem to vanish during winter, they do not hibernate as bears do. They would rather go through a winter rest where they will sleep some of the time, and the rest of the time, will search for the food they stored (caches) during the earlier part of the year. Similar to bears, they also pick up weight and build winter nests. This allows them to be comfortable during the cold months.

Hibernation isn't just done when it is cold. It is also done when there isn't any food or when too many predators are around. The fat-tailed dwarf lemur of

Madagascar will hibernate during summer when there isn't enough food or water to go around. They can hibernate for up to eight months, living off the fat in their tails. Meanwhile, the dormouse, a tiny mouse that lives up to nine years, will hibernate for as long as 10 months to avoid predators from eating it.

And though humans do not hibernate, scientists believe that we can use this behavior to help develop stasis pods for long space journeys in the future. After all, when an animal starts moving after hibernation, its muscles and bones haven't broken down from all that time lying still. There is even the possibility of longer storage for human organs that need to be transplanted. There is still so much we can learn about hibernation and the animals that make it part of their lives.

Night Hag, Demons, and Other Creatures Blamed for Sleep Paralysis

Have you ever woken in the middle of the night and couldn't move or even talk? Did you notice a stranger standing in the corner of your room or at the foot of your bed, and there was nothing you could do? Then you have likely experienced sleep paralysis. Roughly one in five people will experience sleep paralysis in their lifetime. It's a terrifying experience that leaves you feeling anxious and concerned. But it was all a dream, wasn't it?

The science behind sleep paralysis is when you fall asleep, your brain enters the rapid eye movement (REM) stage. This is when you will have your most life-like dreams. To stop you from acting out these dreams, your brain makes some chemicals (neurochemicals) that temporarily paralyze the body. This prevents you from hurting yourself by acting out what's happening in your dream. However, sometimes something goes wrong, and you wake up. The dream is still fresh in your mind,

so fresh that you can still see some of those images. If those images were from a nightmare, you could likely see some scary things. Except there is one problem, your body is still paralyzed, and you cannot react to what your brain is still seeing.

Some signs of sleep paralysis include not being able to speak or move; feeling like you have a great weight on your chest; a feeling of floating, being pulled, or flying; and you may experience hallucinations (seeing things that aren't there). Some people may even experience the feeling that they are not alone as they sleep. Not all hallucinations are traumatic, but as sleep paralysis can be caused by stress and anxiety, it can also cause nightmares. This can cause you to hallucinate horrible things.

Before people understood that this was nothing more than their brain playing tricks on them, they blamed sleep paralysis on many different monsters, demons, and other supernatural occurrences. Different cultures had various stories to explain what was happening, as well as having their own ways to protect people from the monsters.

Those of the Christian faith believed these nighttime disturbances were caused by the demonic creatures known as *incubi* and *succubi*. These creatures looked just like people; except they had clawed feet. Those in Egypt blamed the *jinn*, while in Italy, there was the *Pandafeche*, and in South Africa, the *tokoloshe* and black magic. In some cultures, these creatures were considered a nuisance, while in others there was a chance it could kill you in your sleep. It is believed that the more you fear the supernatural creature, the more dangerous it would be during sleep paralysis. In some cultures, the sudden death of a person while they slept was a sign of something sinister.

During the 1980s, the movie *Nightmare on Elm Street* shared the tale of Freddy Krueger, who could kill people through their dreams. The inspiration for this movie was rooted in what happened to the Hmong people who lived in America during the 1970s and 1980s. These people were originally from Vietnam, but left after the Vietnam war, as they were persecuted for siding with the Americans. At this time, more than 100 men in their Middle Ages died violent and sudden deaths while they were asleep. Doctors believed these men died

due to sudden unexpected nocturnal death syndrome (SUNDS). However, the Hmong people believed these deaths were attributed to a Vietnamese monster named the *Dab Tsog*, also known as the night hag. Those who survived meeting this creature often described her as a tall and pale woman. She would first be noticed at the end of their beds. Then, once noticed, she'd crawl on to the beds and lie upon the men, suffocating them as her weight seemed to grow in time.

This didn't only happen in America but also in Thailand and Singapore, resulting in more than 230 deaths, with the *Dab Tsog* being blamed. To this day, doctors still insist that the deaths were caused by the high levels of stress and anxiety these people felt being in a new country. They were convinced that the new environment, new diet, combined with stress and anxiety, caused these deaths. However, it was strange that most of the deaths were men. This is why so many people still believe in their culture's monsters being the cause of sleep paralysis.

Sleep paralysis can happen to anyone and at any time. It is generally caused by high levels of stress, post-traumatic stress disorder, and even jet lag. You can avoid

suffering from sleep paralysis by following a healthy sleep routine and avoiding sleeping on your back.

A Tangle of Squirrels

When Terry Pratchett wrote *The Amazing Maurice and His Educated Rodents* in 2001, he mentioned a creature named Spider. This creature was unlike any other in his Discworld series as it wasn't just one creature but eight. These eight rats were joined by the tail but had one mind. Spider was a rat king and could control the minds of others around him.

Terry was known to write about fantastic animals and people, and many people believe this is all fantasy. However, rat kings are real and have been seen throughout history from the 16th century up until 2005. In Germany, it was believed that rat kings *(Rattenkönig)* are born when several young rats in one nest become tangled together with items in the nest. Unable to move far, these rats would then be fed by other rats that could move.

Rat kings were thought to be fake because tricksters would glue dead rats together. However, some were not fake but truly accidents affecting these poor animals. There have been 30–60 true rat kings found between 1576 and 2005. Some of which were still alive! It is

usually rare to find a living rat king as they tend to starve to death as they cannot find food as easily for all the hungry mouths.

During the 17th and 18th centuries, the naturists—the scientists at that time—believed that when rat pups were born, their tails became tangled, and the afterbirth would glue them together forever. However, as time moved on and science progressed, this was proved wrong. The truth of rat kings is that rats like to huddle together for warmth, especially in the middle of winter. Substances such as blood, urine, and other liquids would likely freeze on their tails, causing them to become joined. When the rats realize that they're trapped together, they panic and try to pull away. This will cause them to become even more tangled. What proves this theory is that these rat kings are usually found in small, cramped places during the wintertime.

However, rats are not the only animal to get tangled together to form a king. It has also been known to happen to young squirrels. This first occurred in 1951 in the South Carolina Zoo, then again in 2013 (six tangled together), and 2017 with four linked together. And while rat kings are usually terrifying to see, a squirrel

king is saddening. These young squirrels will usually fall from trees and then try to run away but can't pick one direction to run in.

On September 12, 2018, in Wisconsin, a man came across five baby squirrels (greys) tangled together on a pavement trying to escape him. They were scared and tried to bite everyone that wanted to help. Once they were caught, they were taken to the closest wildlife rehabilitation center, where vets tried to untangle them. This was when the vets realized the tangled mess of the five tails was joined with plastic, grass, and twigs. They believed the reason the tails were tangled was that the squirrels had been playing with what was in their nest, causing it to become tangled in their tails, joining them to each other. It took 20 minutes to get the babies separated from each other. However, they were not free to go yet. What had joined them together had caused damage to their tails, and only three of the five still had a bushy tail, while the other two were less bushy. They needed to spend some time getting better.

Then the greys were then taken to the Milwaukee rehabilitation center. Here they were able to run free in a protected area while they recovered from being

joined to their siblings for who knows how many days. They were now able to run separately and not share their food with their other siblings. Can you imagine being joined to your brother or sister and not being able to get away?

The Little Canary and Its Job

As humans advanced, so did their need to fuel their technology. During industrialization (development of industries), there was a greater need for metal and coal to power various industries. This included powering the new steam-powered vehicles. Many materials that helped industrialization were found through mining. However, mining was a dangerous job, and often miners died due to fires, explosions, cave-ins, and the dreaded poisonous gasses, such as carbon monoxide (CO).

Carbon monoxide is an odorless (no smell) and colorless gas which replaces the oxygen in the red blood cells. It is also highly flammable and lighter than air. If someone is poisoned by carbon monoxide, the first signs are feeling dizzy, being short of breath, and having a headache. It would quickly go downhill as the body doesn't get enough oxygen to the different organs, and the person would die. Mines often had carbon monoxide in them because the burning of coal and wood produced it. With more and more demand for coal, metals, and even precious stones, miners were forced to dig deeper into mines, exposing themselves to this gas. They needed to

figure out a way to prevent their deaths.

From 1911 to 1986, the canary was the solution in most mining operations in Britain, America, and Canada. According to John Scott Haldane, the canary would be the perfect animal to help as it is a sentinel species. This means it is a sensitive animal that reacts to changes in its environment quicker than other animals. The canary was chosen over other carriable animals, such as rats, because they have a specialized system of lungs and air sacs. This allowed them to get two breaths of air into their lungs by simply breathing in and out once. The bird would breathe in more air than any other animal and be weak against most gasses. Up to two birds per mining group would go down into the dark to mine coal. They had a special job to complete as they were the first to be affected by the gas.

These were working animals that were well cared for in their cages. Some miners considered them their pets, giving them treats and whistling as they worked. They were often saddened and scared when a canary died because it would only mean one thing: There was gas where they were, and they needed to get out fast. If the miners acted fast enough, they could save the canary's

life. This was done by placing the unconscious canary in a specially designed cage so that oxygen could be pumped into it. Allowing the canary to slowly recover.

In 1926, canaries were being used by rescue teams who had to go into the mines to rescue miners who were trapped after accidents. These birds were used to warn the rescuers about any potential gas pockets that may have been released during the accident. It was during this year that Dugald Macintyre stated that these animals shouldn't be used in mining and that there had to be a better way. Science was failing the birds and the miners.

But as they say, science never stops, and soon an automated system was invented which was able to detect carbon monoxide better than what the birds did. This electronic device was cheaper and more effective. However, the miners continued to use the canaries. The birds had become a part of the mining culture, and the miners were not willing to give up their companions, which had seen them safe for so many years.

By December 30, 1986, British legislation demanded that the miners replace the birds with electronic carbon

monoxide sensors. And so, there was a decline in the use of canaries in mines. Within a year, 200 canaries were retired. That's not to say that canaries were no longer used as some mines continued with the tradition until 1996.

And so ended the hard work by the little yellow bird in the mines. However, it has become a much-loved pet in many homes worldwide, still whistling the tunes that its ancestors sang to those lonely men down in the mines decades ago.

Hubert the Wandering Hippo

This is the story of Hubert, a wandering hippo that left its waterhole in St. Lucia Estuary, Kwazulu Natal, 1928. As to why this hippo started its 1,000-mile walk has left many people scratching their heads. Was it to walk the ancient path of so many hippos before it? Was it looking for the love of their life? Was it frightened because it lost a parent? Whatever the reason, the much-loved hippo wandered its way into the hearts of millions of people, and not just those that called South Africa their home.

For three years, the wandering hippo, called Hubert, wandered along the eastern parts of South Africa. The adventure started when Hubert crossed the Black Umfolozi River. He continued on, enjoying the warm oceans of Durban, crashing parties at country clubs, and even taking midnight dips in any pond that he came across.

Being a mostly herbivorous animal (eats plants), Hubert was often seen eating up gardens, farms, and even golf courses. However, this usually occurred at night as hippos are mostly nocturnal. One of the

most memorable moments of this hippo was when it brought a train to a standstill as it had fallen asleep on the tracks. The train had to use its cattle guard on the front of the train to gently nudge the giant beast awake. It had then wandered away, a little grumpy at being woken up from its nap.

For a time, Hubert settled in the Mhlanga River and was treated as a national hero by anyone who happened to get a glimpse. Visitors often brought gifts of fruit and sugar cane. Due to the popularity of the hippo, several men were tasked with catching it and bringing it to the Johannesburg Zoo. Unfortunately, Hubert was too clever and managed to escape the men. As a result, the hippo was declared a royal game animal. This meant that no one was allowed to catch or hunt it. Hubert was now an international star and became known as South Africa's national pet. By March 1931, Hubert had managed to cross 122 rivers and had come to rest in the Keiskamma River in the Eastern Cape. Unfortunately, this was the final stop for Hubert. A month later, on April 23, 1931, the hippo was found dead, riddled with bullets in the river that had become its home.

There was a public outcry, demanding that justice be

brought to those that killed Hubert. There was even a £200 reward. This was a lot of money in those days, and police were actively searching for the shooter or shooters. It was in May 1931 when the guilty people came forward to admit their fault. These people included most of the Marx family: the father, Nicholaas, his two sons, Petrus and Nicholaas Jr., and a family relative named J. C. Hattingh. According to their testimony, the Marx family spotted large footprints, which led them to a monstrous creature they couldn't identify. They shot the animal, which crossed over onto J. C. Hattingh's farm. J.C. went looking for the so-called 'beast' and found the wounded hippo, which he promptly put out of its misery.

When the four men were told that they had killed a royal game animal they pleaded ignorance as they were illiterate (couldn't read or write) and had no knowledge of the famous hippo. After all, they had to protect their crops from this animal. Despite this, each man was fined £25. This financially ruined the Marx family, who then lost their farm. Both families were shunned by those of the community.

Hubert's body was sent to London to be taxidermied

(stuffed), and this was when it was discovered that Hubert wasn't a boy but rather a girl. An 'a' was added to the name, and the hippo Huberta was returned to South Africa in 1932. This once loved hippo can still be found today in the Amathole Museum in King William's Town, Eastern Cape. Although dead, the story of this wandering hippo and it's amazing journey is still alive in those who have come to know this strange animal. One that decided to walk 1,000 miles from its home to explore the rest of the world.

Harry Wolhuter, the Man Who Survived a Lion Attack

The Kruger National Park, South Africa, is one of the most beautiful nature reserves in the world. It is home to the big five—five of the largest animals known for killing humans. One of these is the largest predator in Africa, the African lion. When you go to the park, you are instructed to stay in the car as it doesn't take a lion much time to catch and drag a human away if not careful.

Few people have survived a full attack by an adult male lion. However, one such man was Harry Wolhuter. This man was one of the first game rangers in the Kruger National Park. His service was from 1902 to 1946. He was a well-liked person who got on well with strangers and the tribal natives of the area, having learned their language. He was considered to have a wide knowledge of the land and its animals; he was an experienced hunter and tracker and was brave and determined. All of this is what led to his survival after he was attacked by a lion in August 1903.

He was traveling on horseback with three other men, donkeys, and three dogs, one unnamed while the other two were named Bull and Fly. He had been scouting olifants (elephants) and now wanted to get to a watering hole so they could rest as night was coming soon. They arrived at the waterhole only to find it dry. They needed water. Harry decided to scout ahead to the next watering hole—about 12 miles away—and it was starting to get dark. It was just him, Bull, and his horse.

Although there were lions in the park, he wasn't worried about them as they were not often seen in the area where he was now. So, as night fell, he wasn't concerned when he heard movement from a clump of tall grass. He expected it to only be a pair of reedbuck, which are common in this area. Unfortunately, it was not a pair of reedbuck, but rather two lions. Realizing his mistake and not having the time to raise his rifle, Harry turned his horse and tried to get away as the lions were preparing to attack. One managed to get hold of the back legs of the horse, which reared, throwing Harry from the saddle. With a tiny bit of luck, Harry landed on top of the second lion, instead of in its mouth. The lion quickly grabbed Harry by his right shoulder and started

dragging him away. The first lion continued to chase the horse, closely followed by Bull.

It was thanks to Harry using the spurs on his shoes to slow them that the lion couldn't run away with its meal. However, each time they moved too slowly, the lion would shake its head, causing Harry pain. Its claws even managed to cut into his arms a few times.

Harry had no gun to save himself from the lion, but he did have a six-inch knife strapped to the back of his belt. He just hoped it was still there after he had fallen from his horse. He used his left hand to reach behind him as he was dragged along on his back, his face pressed into the male's mane. The knife was there! Now he just needed to free himself from the lion's grip. He brought his left arm to stab the lion behind its left shoulder twice. As the lion roared in pain, he managed to stab upwards into its neck. With the serious injury, the lion ran away from Harry.

It had managed to drag Harry 60 yards from where he had fallen. However, he wasn't safe yet. He knew as soon as the first lion realized that it wasn't going to catch the horse, it would be back to eat him.

He had hoped to start a fire, something to scare the remaining lion away, but the dew on the grass prevented this. He only had one other option, and that was to climb a tree. Unfortunately, his right arm was practically useless, and he had to find an easy tree to climb that had a fork that he could reach.

He was weak from blood loss and shock and thought he would fall from the tree. He had to tie himself in place with his belt to prevent that. In the dark, beyond what he could see, he heard the lion he had stabbed groaning in pain before it fell silent. It had died.

Then, the first lion showed up and tracked him to the tree. As the lion was getting ready to climb the tree, Bull showed up and started barking at the lion. A combination of Harry shouting and Bull barking caused the lion to slink away into the darkness. But it wasn't gone yet, it was just waiting for a chance. Harry had to wait in the tree for an hour before the other men traveling with him could find and help him. They got a fire going, which prevented the lion from making its move that night.

However, they were still out of the water, and now

Harry needed it to clean his wounds. They had to keep moving, but this time they had a fire and all three dogs to keep the lion at bay. They eventually came across some huts where they could get some protection, but there still wasn't any water. Harry had to send one of the men ahead to get something as his wounds were so painful that he couldn't walk or even stand anymore. Eventually, they had to resort to using salt to attempt to clean the wounds.

Two of the men returned to where Harry said he had killed the lion, not believing him. They returned not only with his proof but also his horse, which had managed to survive. They returned with the lion's skull, some meat, its heart, and its pelt (skin). They showed Harry how his knife strikes had pierced the lion's heart twice and was the only reason he was still alive. They also stated that the lion's stomach was completely empty and was likely why it had attacked.

From the time of the attack, to when Harry could get medical help—thanks to people in a village nearby that helped carry him—four days had passed. He arrived in Komatipoort with his arm infected and running a high fever. It took months to recover, but eventually, he could

return to duty with a slightly weaker right arm. Despite being attacked by a lion, he never let that get in the way of his passion for Kruger National Park.

Where Did Scarecrows Come From?

The function of these strange things is in its name. It was designed to scare crows—and other animals—away from seeds that had been freshly sowed. It was one of the only ways people could protect their crops without sitting and watching the fields day and night. They have long been in books and movies, such as *Wizard of Oz* and even *Jeepers Creepers.* But where did they come from?

The first known use of a scarecrow was by the Egyptians about 3,000 years ago. It was nothing more than a wooden frame with a net draped over it. This was to protect the wheat from the quail. People would scare the quail, which would then run into the nets, allowing the people to have a tasty snack and protect their harvest.

The next type of scarecrow was used by the ancient Greeks. They would carve statues of the god Priapus— the son of Dionysus and Aphrodite. This god was so ugly, it was said that no bird would be in the same field

as him. The Romans took this belief and made it their own later.

In pre-feudal Japan, they had their own scarecrow called a *kakashi*. This is not the beloved character from *Naruto* but rather a bundle of rags that contained noisemakers such as bells. These were placed on a pole before it was set alight. It is said that the smell and sight of the flames chased animals away. Later, the farmers adapted this practice and created man-like shapes by having a frame wear a hat and a coat. Sometimes the scarecrow was made more fearsome with the addition of a weapon.

In Europe during the Middle Ages, children were hired by the farmer to chase birds away using two blocks to make a lot of noise. However, after the Black Plague, there weren't many children, and the farmers had to become creative to save their crops. They used turnips or pumpkins to make the head, then stuffed clothes with straw to give the appearance of a body and hung this in their fields. This looked like a man at a distance, and animals were wary of coming too close.

Native Americans had their own versions of scarecrows. Sometimes this was simply a man sitting on a raised

platform who would scare off birds by shouting at them. Other times, several poles were connected with a cord that was draped with animal skins. These would move in the wind, scaring animals. As time progressed and Europeans moved into America, the idea of the scarecrow would change again.

The Germans brought the *bootzamon* (bogeyman), which would stand at the edges of fields. Occasionally it would be joined by a female version on the other side of the field.

However, the heyday of the scarecrow was soon over with the discovery of pesticides (poisons) such as DDT. These chemicals made it easier to deal with all pests, from insects to birds. Nowadays, you will only find scarecrows in private gardens, rural communities, and certain holidays such as Halloween. It is as if the human-like protector of crops finally has a chance to retire and enjoy some downtime.

How Were the Pyramids Built?

There are many theories about how the pyramids were built. Some believe aliens did it, while others believe it was done by the people of the lost city of Atlantis. Others also insist that it was slaves or farmers. The truth; however, was much different.

There are over 100 different pyramids scattered throughout Egypt. Some had stepped sides, as those made for Pharaoh Djoser. While others had smooth sides, as seen with those created for Pharaoh Snefru. However, pharaohs eventually stopped building these monuments between 1550 and 1070 B.C.E., in favor of being buried in the Valley of Kings.

Some of the greatest pyramids were the Pyramids of Giza, three large pyramids that are clustered together. The largest of these, the Great Pyramid, took 23 years to build, stood almost 500 feet tall, and needed 2.3 million stones to complete. Amazing, yes? What is more amazing is that the Egyptians could do this using copper tools and no wheels. How these marvels were built is a secret that was taken to the grave. However, some scientists can make a few guesses while the rest has

been discovered through science and archeology (study of human history).

First, the stones used in the pyramids were limestone that were mined in Giza and granite. The granite was mined roughly 620 miles away and was transported along the Nile. These stones were large and weighed a lot. With no wheels, it seemed impossible to transport them from the Nile to the building site. However, the Egyptians were clever. They used sleds to pull the stones to the building site. They discovered that just the right amount of water to make the desert sands slick caused less friction, allowing the sled to move easier as it was pulled by animals and people. As most of the stones would be used in the base of the pyramid, it is believed that a wide ramp was used to move the stones upward. As the pyramid grew in height—and needed fewer stones—this ramp would have become narrower and wrapped around the outside of the structure.

Scientists believe there was a working force of 1,200–1,500 men that worked in shifts to complete the work of the Great Pyramid. This rotating labor force was made up of several teams according to graffiti found around the building sites. These teams were identified

with names such as Friends of Khufu and Drunkards of Menkaure. With some translation work done on some discovered papyrus manuscripts, it was also discovered a work gang of about 200 men was led by one named Merer. This team didn't just work on the pyramids but other structures throughout Egypt.

Although it isn't sure whether these men were seasonal or permanent workers, it is a fact that they, and others working on the pyramids, were well treated. Large cities have been excavated (dug up) that housed large numbers of people that likely lived there while the pyramids were built. These areas showed signs of bread being baked and beer brewed daily. There were also signs of thousands of animals being butchered and eaten by those who lived here. Merer's men weren't only well-fed, but they were also compensated with textiles, perhaps as a form of payment.

This leads historians to believe that these were not slaves building these pyramids but rather skilled laborers who were clearly rewarded for their hard work. This was proved by bodies dug up close to the pyramid in worker cemeteries. These bodies showed signs of a respectful burial. Some even had old injuries, which were treated

and showed signs of healing. This indicated medical care had been given to them. Working on the pyramids was seen as an honor, and these people were treated well and fed like royalty.

With research still discovering new pieces of information yearly, soon we will know the truth of the pyramids and how they were built. Until then, we mostly have theories and bits and pieces of information to keep us going.

History of Prosthetics

The loss of a body part is usually traumatic and scary. Not only because of how it happened, but also because of what we think others will think of us. Humans have lost nonfunctional and functional parts of their bodies for as long as they have been around. These body parts were often replaced to help these people feel whole and normal again. In the past, not being whole was seen as a deformity, and needed to be covered up or fixed as soon as possible. These missing body parts were replaced with prosthetics.

The earliest prosthetic was discovered in Shahr-I Sokhta in the southeastern part of Iran. The body dated back to 2900 B.C.E., and it was an eye prosthetic that fitted to the outside of a woman's eye socket. This almost round clay object was coated in gold and had two tiny holes on either side. It is believed that gold thread was put through it to allow the wearer to wear the eye daily. The wear and tear on this person's eye socket showed that she wore this eye for some time before her death.

Clay was a common material used to make replacements for eyes. This remained unchanged until

the 16th century when the Venetians started creating glass eyes. However, these didn't always sit well, were uncomfortable, and would often shatter.

Then, in the mid-19th century, the Germans used their glassblowing skills to create more comfortable glass eyes. However, during WWII, it became difficult to get replacement eyes, causing the Americans to make their own by using acrylic plaster. This was a stronger material that was more comfortable and didn't break easily. Today, this acrylic plastic is still used. However, it is now easier to match the eye color of your remaining eye in comparison to what was done in the past.

The eye was hardly the only part of the body that needed to be replaced. The next oldest prosthetic was known as the Cairo Toe. This was a wooden, life-like toe that was fitted to an Egyptian noblewoman somewhere between 950–710 B.C.E. It was so life-like, that it even had a nail carved into it. This wooden toe was stained and was held in place with a series of leather threads. It is believed that this woman had the toe made because it was easier for her to walk with the sandals they had available about 3,000 years ago. In general, prosthetics made people's lives easier and allowed them to be who

they wanted to be.

The first person to be named who wore prosthetics was Marcus Sergius Silus, a Roman general who lived from 240–187 B.C.E. During the second Punic war, he was severely injured and lost his right hand. However, he never gave up on his career and had a hand made from iron that could hold onto his shield. Even missing his biological hand, he could continue to fight in wars. He even sustained another 23 injuries in his long career.

As wars progressed around the world, different weapons were invented that would cut and pulverize limbs, which resulted in amputations so the victim would survive. Because being without a limb was considered shameful and unsightly during these times, knights would often have blacksmiths make them new arms, which were part of their armor. These metal limbs would look life-like but they were generally only used to hide what was lost, and rarely had any functionality. By the Middle Ages, there was no advancement in prosthetics. Replacement limbs during this time were all similar to what General Marcus used.

However, by the 16th century, Doctor Ambroise Paré

invented the hinged hand and a leg with a hinged knee that could lock as a person walked. These prosthetics were adjustable and more lightweight than their previous metal ancestors because they were made with leather, paper, and glue. He wanted the limbs to not only look like the real thing but to move like them as well. He also revolutionized the technique which allowed for the attachment of the prosthetics.

By 1690, Pieter Verdyn created a lower leg prosthetic—where a person still had their own knee but nothing below it—which made it easier to wear. In 1800, James Potts made an above-knee prosthetic with a socket between the calf and thigh. Not only that, but the foot was articulate (moveable), giving the limb life-like characteristics. This continued to be the standard leg replacement all the way to the American Civil War, which was fought between 1861 and 1865.

On June 1, 1861, James Hanger joined his brothers to fight in the Civil War as a soldier. On June 3, 1861, he was struck by a cannonball and lost his left leg. He became the first amputee of the Civil War. Miraculously he survived the amputation and returned to his family home in August, where he remained in his room until

later that year. His family believed him to be grieving his leg, but they were wrong. By November that year, he walked down the stairs, much to the amazement of his family. He had created a new leg from barrel staves and metal. This leg contained a hinge at the knee and ankle, allowing James to walk with more comfort than other prosthetics of the age. James then went on to create the J. E. Hanger Company—now known as Hanger, Inc.—which is still one of the forerunners of the prosthetic market today!

Even after all this time and modernization, prosthetics, although giving people a new lease on life, were uncomfortable and even painful for some people. This was alleviated by better amputation practices and the invention of the suction sock by U. C. Berkeley in 1946 for lower limb amputations.

The use of prosthetics for athletes has also changed how prosthetics are viewed and created. The blade prosthetic was invented in the 1970s by Van Phillips. This artificial limb allowed people to run and not just walk. Up until this point, most prosthetics were made to hide the missing limbs and were as life-like as possible.

Further advancement was made in 1975 when Ysidro M. Martinez moved away from the natural look and started to improve on the gait (how a person walks) and lowered the amount of friction between the prosthetic and the person's body, which improved the comfort of wearing a prosthetic.

Nowadays, limbs of all kinds can be 3D printed. Not only can they be as life-like as possible, but they are more affordable and more comfortable. Who knows what the future can bring? Perhaps there is a chance that medical science can develop a biomechanical (biological and artificial) limb that can grow with a person instead of getting a new prosthetic every few years.

Douglas Bader, Double-Leg Amputee WWII Ace Pilot

World War II lasted from 1939 to 1945 and resulted in some of the most terrible things seen by man. However, it wasn't all bad. Discoveries were made at this time, including the discovery of penicillin, the development of flu shots, and the invention of the jet engine. This was also the time of heroes. This included those of the Axis powers and the Allied powers.

One of those heroes was Sir Douglas Bader. He was an ace pilot for the Royal Air Force (RAF) with medals such as the Distinguished Service Order and the Distinguished Flying Cross. With 23 confirmed downed German aircraft, he was named the fifth deadliest RAF ace. What made all of this even more amazing was he could achieve all of this as a double amputee.

Douglas was a very athletic child, but with the death of his father during WWI, he needed a scholarship just to go to school. It was thanks to this he was eventually able to get a cadetship at the Cranwell Air Force Academy in 1928. Within two years, he had graduated and started

flying for the RAF. Unfortunately, it wasn't to last.

During an acrobatic display, he flew too close to the ground and crashed his plane. He was so severely injured the doctors had no choice but to remove both his legs. One above the knee, and the other below. Even with the loss of his legs, Douglas wasn't willing to give up. With a lot of work, he was able to walk again with his new tin prosthetics (fake legs), he even had a car specially made for him so he could still drive. However, despite all this, he was forced to leave the RAF. He was told that he could return if war was ever declared again.

When war was declared in 1939, he returned to active duty. Some people tried to keep him out of a plane, but he successfully completed his refresher course and was allowed to fly once more. In 1940, he came face-to-face with the Spitfire in Duxford, England, which would later become his plane.

Even with his fake legs, he was soon flying combat missions. It was during the Evacuation of Dunkirk that he shot down his first German plane. This wasn't the only time he was part of events crucial to the war. To prevent the invasion of Britain between 1940 and 1941,

he and Trafford Leigh-Mallory worked together on the Big Wing strategy. At this time, Douglas shot down 22 more German planes. However, his luck soon ran out.

August 9, 1941, he was captured by the Germans after his plane accidentally hit a Messerschmitt 109, and he was forced to parachute out. Unfortunately, his right leg was caught in the plane as it fell. Thankfully, the leather strap, which kept his leg attached to him, snapped, allowing Douglas to get free. Luckily for him, he was quite famous, even among the Germans. Because of this, they treated him a lot better than any other prisoners of war. This gave Douglas plenty of opportunities to try and escape with only a single leg. Despite all his escape attempts, the Germans would fix his damaged right leg and later asked for a replacement leg to be sent.

Yet, no matter how well they treated the ace pilot, he continued trying to escape. His escapes became so numerous, Hitler eventually had him sent to Colditz castle in 1942. This castle was thought to be an inescapable prison, yet Douglas still tried, and even succeeded in, escaping a few times. However, it was becoming more and more difficult. Eventually,

he settled on making the guards' lives difficult with shouting matches and other hijinks.

After three years of his imprisonment in the castle, he was eventually rescued in 1945. With the war nearing its end, Douglas found that he had lost his taste for flying with the RAF. Eventually, he would retire and accept a job with the Shell Oil Company. He flew between Europe and North Africa and was in charge of public relations.

Douglas was the kind of man who believed that you should never believe people who say you can't do something. After all, he was the man named the fifth deadliest ace, escaped German-controlled lands, and learned to drive a car, all without the legs he was born with. He truly is someone to look up to.

Corgis and the Fairy Folk

If you have ever seen Queen Elizabeth II, you have likely seen her faithful companions, Pembroke Welsh corgis. This unique dog has a history as strange as its appearance. Some people believe that the dog was brought with the Flemish weavers in the 12th century. While others believe it came with the Scandinavian raiders. If you look at the Swedish vallhund, you will see that the corgi is almost the same, yet not quite.

The corgi is a working dog and was bred to be a cattle herder. Because of its small size, it easily dodged the flying hooves of angry cows while it would bite at the animals to move them through the fields. Where did this cute dog come from, and why does it love humans so much?

The Welsh have many stories about the corgi and their bond with fairies. The legends say that the fairies had wings that were not strong enough to carry them long distances. This made them lazy, and fairies didn't want to travel far. They needed something that would help them travel fast and were loyal and friendly, so they made the corgi.

The word corgi means dwarf dog in Welsh, explaining their size, which was perfect for the fairy folk. This little dog was used not only for fairy travel, but also to pull their wagons and carriages, and they were even ridden into battle. If you look between the shoulders of a light-colored corgi, you can make out a dark patch of fur where the saddle used to sit.

However, all this work was only during the day. Since the fairies had no use for the corgi at night, they would send the friendly dogs into villages close to where they lived. These dogs would play and watch over children, and only return to their masters when the sun rose. So how did the dogs come to live with people? Well, there are two stories.

The first involved the king and queen of the fairies. One day they were traveling with their corgis when they found some people working hard in the fields. All the people ever did was work and never had time to do anything fun or relax. This sight was so depressing that the king fell from his corgi. The queen jumped from her corgi to make sure he was alright.

The two corgis continued without realizing their

passengers had been left behind. The King was worried the corgis would get lost because they were on their own. However, the wise Queen said that they wouldn't be lost for long, that soon the humans would find them. The queen continued by saying that they didn't really need the dogs; but clearly, the humans could.

The dogs continued to play as they traveled, eventually attracting the attention of several children. These children continued to play with the dogs until night came. They took the dogs back to their farm, where the father stated that these were dwarf dogs that were often used by fairies. He continued by saying since they were now on the farm, they were clearly a gift from the fairies, and they should use them. From that day forth, the corgis worked on the farm with the family, helping with the cattle and playing now and again to allow the people to rest.

A slightly different tale tells of a war between the *Tylwyth Teg* and the *Gwyllion* fairy tribes. Corgis had been their working animals, but now they were going to become battle steeds. Supposedly, these animals were resistant to magic and would be difficult to target with it. During the war, two *Tylwyth Teg* riders were killed. To

honor them, their friends had a ceremony to bury them.

Two children stumbled across this ceremony, interrupting the fairies. Overcome with sadness, the fairies explained what they were doing and gave the children the two corgis, which had been the fairies' mounts. They explained that the animals made wonderful steeds but were better as helpers on the farms as they were small enough not to get kicked by most animals.

Whether the majestic corgi was brought, or bred, or given to us by the fairy folk, we will never truly know. All we do know is that the corgi is a wonderfully friendly, loyal, and hard-working dog that is steeped in mystery and a little magic.

Why Wales Have a Dragon on Its Flag

A country's flag means something to its people. Each one is unique and different, telling the tale of the country. However, if you look at the flags, any animal that is on one, is one that we can see in nature. This is not so for the Welsh flag, which contains a red dragon. The history of *Y Ddraig Goch* (meaning red dragon) is ancient, starting during the 4th century and finally being recognized as the national flag in 1959.

The use of the red dragon (Draco) was first seen in the 4th century. It was seen on the banners of the Romano-British soldiers as they marched toward Rome. This dragon would appear once more as a symbol by the Welsh Kings of Aberffraw when the Romans left Britain in the 5th century. It would later be adopted as the emblem for King Cadwaladr (Cadwallader) of Gwynedd in 655 C.E.

But was this a true dragon? The Welsh used the word *draig*, a symbol of strength, and was used to describe a strong leader. It was believed that this *draig* would be

the one to free the Welsh from English rule. This word would later be joined with the symbol of the dragon. The Welsh didn't see the dragon as something to be feared but rather, had a positive relationship with it. Many heroes were considered dragon-like.

This red dragon also had links to the legends of King Arthur. Merlin had a prophecy about a white dragon fighting a red dragon. It is believed that the red dragon represented the Anglo-Saxons (the people who would become the modern-day Welsh) and the white dragon the English. The white dragon was meant to represent Uther Pendragon, the father of Arthur. Coincidentally, Pendragon means the dragon's head.

The red dragon would surface now and again throughout the history of the Welsh. However, it was Henry Tudor (later King Henry VII) who joined the red dragon to his family colors of green and white after he defeated King Richard III in the 15th century. This happened during the Battle of Bosworth in 1485.

Dragons were viewed as creatures to be feared and used to strike terror in the hearts of one's foes. This may have been one reason Henry used the image of a

dragon. However, many people believed he was trying to prove his lineage (family line) to old King Cadwaldr.

Y Ddraig Goch has been with the Welsh people for centuries. For political reasons, however, the red dragon upon the Welsh flag was not recognized by anyone as a national flag. It took the Queen of England (Queen Elizabeth II) agreeing to it in 1959 for it to officially be the national flag flown over the Welsh government buildings.

Today the Welsh flag has a background that is half white at the top and half green at the bottom. In the center is a red dragon with a single raised claw, a long snake-like tongue, two large wings, and a curled tail. This image is surrounded by the words *Y Ddraig Goch Ddyry Cychwyn.* This can translate to mean 'the red dragon gives impetus' or 'the red dragon inspires action'. It is officially the oldest national flag still flown today, despite only being recognized as a national flag since 1959.

Ching Shih, the World's Most Notorious Pirate

Pirates have existed for centuries, capturing our imaginations with stories such as *Pirates of the Caribbean* and *Treasure Island,* just to name a few. They were found in all corners of the world, plundering (stealing) anything they could find. It is well known that most pirates were male because in the West, women on ships were considered bad luck, and no one would have them aboard. However, this was not true in the East. This is likely what led to the rise of Ching Shih, the most successful female pirate the world had ever seen. At the height of her success, she was in charge of over 80,000 men and women, 1,800 large junks (a type of ship), and about 800 smaller ships. But who was this woman, and how did she rise to control such a large force?

It all started in 1801, when the pirate Zheng Yi (Cheng Yi), the commander of the Red Flag Fleet, married a 26-year-old Ching Shih (also known as Zheng Yi Sao, born as Shih Yang). It is believed that she only married him once he promised to give her 50% of the money he owned and some control over his pirate fleet. Others

believe he kidnapped her and forced her to marry him.

Cheng himself was quite famous in the South China Sea because he was able to unite many rival pirate groups under his name, growing the strength of his fleet and the power he had. Despite being a woman, Ching Shih was a shrewd businesswoman who handled the finances of the fleet and took equal control in piracy beside her husband. At this stage, Cheng had about 200 ships under his control.

For six years, the two of them amassed a large following, until Cheng died in 1807 at the age of 42. This left Ching Shih in a strange situation. First, the crew was not used to a woman leading them, and second, Cheng had a son. This son, Cheung Po Tsai, was adopted by Cheng as an adolescent and was the rightful heir to the Red Flag Fleet. Ching Shih wasn't ready to give up the power she had worked so hard to build with Cheng. She did the only thing she could think of to stay in power: She married her adopted stepson, then continued to keep the power she had enjoyed with her first husband.

With her rule now cemented, she and Cheung Po Tsai continued to grow their crew. Soon they were

controlling over 80,000 people (male and female) under a single flag. Despite the sheer numbers Ching Shih controlled, she never lost her power because she used a series of codes that kept everyone in check. If someone gave orders which were not from a superior, or if they ignored orders from superiors, they were punished with death, which came swiftly. She even had rules on how captive women were to be treated and not hurt in any way, under the penalty of death or banishment. The crew may not have liked her very much, but they respected her and continued to follow her.

For three years under Ching Shih's rule, the Red Flag Fleet managed to outsmart and outmaneuver the East India Company, the Portuguese Navy, and the Qing dynasty officials.

However, in 1810, the crew of the Red Flag Fleet was starting to come undone. The leaders of the Black Flag, a crew under the Red Flag Fleet, surrendered to those chasing after them. As these pirates made up a large portion of Ching's fleet, she knew her crew wouldn't last too much longer without the Black Flag crew. Ching decided it was best to follow the Black Flag Fleet. She was granted amnesty by the Chinese government and

Emperor and retired from her pirate life.

Although Ching passed away in 1844 at the ripe old age of 69, she would never be forgotten. If you are a fan of the *Pirates of the Caribbean: At World's End,* you may remember one of the nine Pirate Lords was a woman named Mistress Ching. This fictional pirate was a dedication to the life of Ching Shih as one of the most notorious pirates who existed.

Fairies, Hoax or Not?

Many countries worldwide have stories of creatures that inhabit the world with us. One of the more famous creatures is fairies. Many myths and legends surround these mysterious creatures, but there has never been real proof of their existence. That was, until July 1917 when two cousins named Elsie Wright and Frances Griffith stunned the world with several photographs of these sprites.

It all started when the girls asked Elsie's father (Arthur Wright) if they could use his camera to take some photos of the fairies around Cottingley. The man thought it was a joke but still showed the girls how to use the camera, then let them go play. They returned a few hours later, smiling, saying they had been successful.

Once the photos were developed, there indeed were several fairy-like creatures that seemed to be playing with the girls. Arthur was still convinced that this was a joke but kept the photos. A month later, the girls took another photo, but this time it was of Elsie with a gnome-like creature.

Polly Wright (mother to Elsie) didn't believe this to be a joke though. She took the pictures with her to a lecture on spiritualism (the belief of being able to communicate with the beyond) in 1919. Polly was convinced the girls had taken a photo of the supernatural and wanted to share it with like-minded people. She asked the speaker, Edward Gardner, what he thought of the images. He then turned to a photographer named Harold Snelling to get his opinion. Harold took a look at the photos and declared them to be the real thing. Now that the images had been proven real, they spread to the rest of the spiritualism community.

These images eventually found their way to Sir Arthur Conan Doyle (author of the Sherlock Holmes books). He was so convinced these images were real, that he went to see the two girls himself and asked if they could get him a few more. Elsie and Frances did just that and gave him another three photos in August 1920. Sir Arthur then went on to write an article about how these photographs proved the existence of the supernatural.

As these images and various articles started circulating, it caused fighting between the spiritualists and those that couldn't believe what they were seeing. The

skeptics were convinced the photos were fake! And they were right, but it took a few decades for them to be debunked (proved fake).

In 1978, James Randi pointed out that the so-called "fairies" looked exactly like the fairies in the book titled *Princess Mary's Gift Book,* which had been published just before 1915, shortly before the girls started taking photos of their fairies. However, it wasn't till 1981, that Elsie Wright admitted this was true and all the photos were indeed fake. Turns out that they had used paper cutouts from the book and arranged them to create the so-called "magical" photos.

With a modern eye, it is easy to see these photos were fakes. However, back then, many people desperately wanted to prove the existence of the supernatural. This caused them to overlook clues that could have helped them see through the fakes. The photos of the fairies were images of an unseen world, and people were curious. What may have started out as a trick by two young girls had to become a bigger lie as time passed. Perhaps the girls felt they had no other choice and continued their lie. Although Elsie admitted the photos were fake, Frances insisted that the final picture they

took was of a real fairy. We will never know the truth, and until we do, we can only believe deep in our hearts that fairies exist.

The History of the Teddy Bear

The Teddy Bear is one of the most well-loved of all toys ever invented. It is the friend that is always willing to cuddle and protect us from the things that hide in the dark. Yet, how did a bear—one of the most dangerous predators in the world—become a well-loved toy? Well, it all started with an argument in 1902.

The union for the United Mine Workers of America arranged for all of their workers to go on strike (when workers refuse to work). They wanted to work shorter days and for more money.

Unfortunately, there was a surplus (too much) of coal, and the mines were not making enough money. The mine company couldn't legally close the various mines. For this reason, the strike was actually working in the company's favor. They didn't have to pay the workers, since they were striking, and with the remaining supply of coal starting to run out, they would be able to drive up the price.

There seemed to be no end to the struggle between the union representatives and the mine owners. With

no coal being mined, it was starting to look as if it could possibly be a cold winter.

It became such a big problem that President Theodore Roosevelt threatened to send his troops to the Midwest to take over the anthracite (hard coal) mines. He met with the union leaders and the mine owners in the fall to reach an agreement. As the nightly temperatures started to fall, so did their tempers, and soon they agreed on a deal that benefited both parties.

With all the hard work behind him, Roosevelt felt that he needed a vacation. He accepted an invitation to go hunting with Governor Andrew Longino in Mississippi. During this time, there were a lot of racial tensions between white Americans and African Americans. Andrew hoped that by inviting Roosevelt to visit, he would be able to prevent the infighting between the two races which was threatening.

Roosevelt joined Andrew on a bear hunt in November 1902. They were hardly alone! With them were 50 dogs, many horses, lots of trappers and photographers, and an ex-slave by the name of Holt Collier.

Holt was an excellent guide who had been a cavalryman

during the Civil War, and he knew the land well. He was also an expert on hunting bears, having hunted and killed many in the past. He had been hired by Andrew because of his skills at hunting in dangerous, swampy land for large animals. Roosevelt couldn't have been in safer hands.

This hunting trip was meant to last 10 days. Roosevelt wanted a bear by the first day, but this didn't happen. However, by the second day, the hunting dogs had caught the scent of a bear. They spent most of the day tracking and hunting the animal before it was cornered by Holt's dogs. It was an old black bear, barely weighing 230 pounds, but it knew how to defend itself. It wasn't long before it had managed to kill some of Holt's dogs. Fearing for his hounds, the man blew on his bugle to alert the other hunters of his position. Then, he hit the bear over the head with his rifle, and while the bear was stunned, he tied it to a tree.

When the other huntsmen arrived, they all cheered Roosevelt on to get him to shoot the bear tied to the tree. However, despite being a hunter, Roosevelt had a soft spot for animals, and refused to shoot the bear, even after it was no longer tied up. He felt that

it was unsportsmanlike and not becoming of a man. Eventually, the bear was killed with a knife by another hunter and Holt, before it was taken back to camp.

News of what Roosevelt did spread, and on November 17, 1902, cartoonist Clifford K. Berryman drew his iconic cartoon. This cartoon contained Roosevelt in his rough rider uniform, turning his back on a collared black bear cub that looked terrified. It was titled *Drawing the Line in Mississippi,* and it appeared in the *Washington Post.* Some people believed this comic strip was more than just him refusing to shoot a bear. It was about him refusing to take part in the violence against the African American people. Regardless of the intent, Clifford continued to draw small, cute bears in all his political cartoons that contained Roosevelt while he was president.

While the rest of the world admired Roosevelt's sportsmanship, Rose and Morris Michtom saw an opportunity. This Russian-Jewish immigrant couple ran a small store that sold a variety of items. However, soon their display window would have a new addition: a plush, velvet toy in the shape of a bear. Dozens of people saw the bear and wanted to buy it. However,

the Michtom's were hesitant as they weren't sure if they were allowed to. They sent the original bear to Roosevelt and asked if they could name their creation after him. He agreed and so the Teddy Bear was born.

The toy became so popular that the couple had to get out of the candy business and only make stuffed bears. They founded the Ideal Novelty and Toy Company and continued to make toys for years to come. Due to the toy's popularity, Roosevelt even made it the symbol of the 1904 Republican Party. Despite many other kinds of plush toys available, the Teddy Bear is still one of the most popular toys for children and will likely continue to be so for years to come.

Just Nuisance, the Royal Navy Great Dane

In Simon's Town, in Cape Town, South Africa, there is a bronze statue in Jubilee Square showing a large dog. However, this isn't just any dog; this is a Great Dane, one of the largest and tallest dogs in the world. This is Just Nuisance, an Able Seaman of the Royal Navy from 1939–1944, and he was one of the most beloved dogs in the service.

This Great Dane was born April 1, 1937, to parents Koning (King) and Diana and was registered as Pride of Rondebosch—which was his original name before it was later changed. The breeder, H. Bosman then sold the pup to Benjamin Chaney and his wife before they moved to Simon's Town. Benjamin ran the United Services Institute (USI), a hostel for sailors who stayed onshore. This hostel was often visited by the Royal Navy sailors because the naval base was run by the Royal Navy at this time.

The Great Dane puppy grew large—as Danes do—and it didn't help that the sailors would often sneak him some

tasty treats and beer most of the time. In time, the dog would learn to recognize the bell-bottom trousers and the square blue collars of the sailors. Other servicemen without these uniforms were not readily approached.

As the dog grew, he started following the sailors as they went about their daily jobs. Often, this included going onto ships that were in the harbor. One of his favorite vessels was the HMS *Neptune*. He would often be found sleeping at the top of the gangway, making it difficult to climb over him if anyone needed to get onto the ship. Since he hated being woken and moved, he created quite a nuisance of himself and that is how the name stuck.

Yet, it wasn't only onto the ships that Nuisance would follow his sailor friends; he would also ride the train with them. He would often travel through all 27 train stations (22 miles) throughout Cape Town, getting on and off at various stations when it suited him.

Despite the sailors trying to hide him from the ticket collectors, which was hard because he took up three seats, he was often removed from the train. Yet, this didn't stop him from riding the train. He would wait for

the next train or walk to the next station to take the following one.

However, the railway officials were tired of a dog taking up so many seats. They told his owner that they would have him put down unless his fare was paid, or was locked up, or the owner had to get rid of him.

There was such a public and naval outcry about this that letters started to pour into the navy, begging them to do something, and something they did do!

The Royal Naval was expecting WWII to happen soon, and they needed every sailor that was willing to volunteer. So, they accepted Nuisance as a volunteer. As an enlisted sailor, Nuisance was entitled to free rail travel whenever he wanted, as long as he had his pass, which was attached to a specially made collar. He officially enlisted on August 25, 1939.

But there was a slight problem; He didn't have a proper name! He was registered as Pride of Rondebosch, but everyone called him Nuisance; he had no first name. After a short debate, the paperwork was completed. His full name was Just Nuisance, and his occupation was "bone crusher." He signed all the paperwork with

his paw print, and it was official; he was an Ordinary Seaman. However, he was soon promoted to Able Seaman due to his previous service for breaking up fights between sailors. He was, after all, when standing on his back legs, over 6-feet tall. He also had a habit of returning drunk sailors found on the train home. This included sailors who were not stationed at Simon's Town!

He was considered a superstar that not only helped with the morale of the troops during WWII, but he also made a contribution to funding the war. He was "married" to another Great Dane named Adinda, and she had five pups. Two of these pups, Victor and Wilhelmina, were auctioned off to raise funds. Just Nuisance's image was also printed on several postcards, and a book was released about him.

Unlike other sailors, Just Nuisance never set sail. However, he would often fly in a Fairy Fulmer to help spot submarines. And before you think Just Nuisance was a good boy, he wasn't always. He actually had a conduct sheet that detailed some of his worst behaviors. This included sleeping in Petty officer's beds when he was just an Able Seaman and killing two other ship's

mascots in fights. Some of his punishments included not getting any bones for a week.

Sadly, during his earlier life, Just Nuisance had been in a car accident, which caused thrombosis that slowly started to paralyze him. He was discharged from his sailor duties on January 1, 1944. There was nothing anyone could do for him, and on his seventh birthday, April 1, 1944, he was put to sleep. However, the next day not only was he buried with full military colors, he also had a bugler and a firing squad.

The legacy of this amazing companion and sailor still remains. The Simon's Town Museum has a whole section dedicated to him. Plus, there is a yearly parade dedicated to him on April 1. This is when people can bring their Great Danes to see which best resemble the Able Seaman. He may be gone, but he will never be forgotten.

Why the Great Wall of China Was Built

The Great Wall of China is the longest human-made thing at 13,170.70 miles long. Its average height is 20–23 feet and at its highest it is 46-feet. It is 2,700 years old, and over one million people have worked on it from its first day of construction. It is truly a marvel of human architecture, but why was it built? The answer depends on when this question is asked as it was used as a border defense, a way to defend against the nomad tribes in the north, and for tourism.

When the wall's construction started, it wasn't meant to be as long as it is now. It was a series of smaller walls used to defend various pieces of land. Before China became one country in 221 B.C.E., various princes and overlords fought over the land they had, wanting to grow their territory by claiming more. It is believed that the very first section of the wall was built in 656 B.C.E. during the spring and fall by Qi Huangong. The reason he did this was to protect his land from possible invasion by the Chu State. Other states saw this and then started building their own walls to prevent invasions from their

enemies. The Qin, Zhao, and Yan state walls were built in the 4th century B.C.E.

After the unification, the first Chinese emperor, Qin Shihuang, had the three northern walls joined into one. Why these walls were joined isn't really known, but people believe it is because of a rumor the emperor heard. The emperor was obsessed with ruling forever, so he sent a necromancer, Lu Sheng, to discover a way to become immortal. They never discovered how to do this, but Lu Sheng whispered a rumor in the emperor's ear: He would be dethroned by the nomads of the north. To prevent this rumor from becoming true, the emperor ordered the walls joined.

Those who lived in the north had arid land, and they wanted to get to the rich farmlands to the south. In later years, they would attack those on the other side of the wall. This wall was meant to separate the rest of China from the so-called "ungovernable" tribes. It provided enough protection as the northern tribes didn't dare go around it to the west, as that was where the desert was, and to the east was the ocean.

Over time, the wall would be continually strengthened

by Han Gaozu (2020 B.C.E.) and lengthened. The Great Wall was extended to the Yumen Pass and joined with the Dunhuang Wall by Emperor Hun Wudi (141–87 B.C.E.). For three following dynasties from 581–1279 (Sui, Tang, and Song), people continued to rebuild, extend, and modify the wall to protect the Chinese empire from possible northern invaders.

There was no building on the Great Wall during the Yuan Dynasty (1279–1368) as the Mongols had invaded and had taken over China. This was all thanks to Genghis Khan. However, the Chinese managed to take back their land, and the Ming Dynasty lasted from 1368 to 1644. This was a period of strengthening and building the wall once more. During this time, it extended from Jiayuguan to Shanhaiguan. This was the last time the wall would be built on.

From 1644 to 1911 (Qing Dynasty), the people felt that the wall had already served its purpose and there was no use in spending money or resources on it. Since there was no longer a reason to extend the wall, starting in 1957, China decided parts should be maintained, allowing tourists to see it every year.

About a third of the Great Wall is no longer around for us to see. This is because of theft of the stones and little maintenance in certain areas. It is also considered the world's longest cemetery. Over 1 million people worked on its construction and many of the bodies of those who died became buried among the stones.

Lastly, to put rumors to rest, you cannot see the Great Wall from space. So, it is best to go see it for yourself one day to marvel at the amount of work accomplished over the centuries.

The 'Doctor' Who Saved
Thousands of Premature Babies

Sometimes babies are born before they are ready. Children born more than 3 weeks before their due date are called premature babies or preemies. Today, these babies can be placed in incubators and get a lot of attention from the doctors and nurses in hospitals. However, this wasn't always the case. In the past, the incubator wasn't readily available, or doctors weren't willing to use it. This caused many preemies to die due to being underdeveloped and underweight. It cost a lot of money to save these children, who were often considered weaklings by doctors. But it wasn't just the invention of the incubator that saved thousands of premature babies. It was the man who made them into a sideshow that saved their lives and still saves lives today.

It all started in 1881 with Stéphane Étienne Tarnier in France, who worked with many premature babies. He is credited with the first infant warming device, and he wanted to use it in a hospital. He got the inspiration for his idea from the Russian doctor Johann Georg von

Rueg, who used a warming tube, and Carl Siegmund Fraz Credé, who made a double-walled crib that circulated hot water. However, Étienne was largely ignored as many considered his version of an incubator to be too unscientific.

Then there was Piere Budin, who started his research into using incubators in 1888. However, he too struggled to get support for his idea. He decided he needed to show his idea to the world. He did this by showing living babies in incubators in the 1896 Berlin's World Fair. This is when Martin Couney saw the incubators for the first time and realized that this was perfect for saving premature babies. Not only that, but people were paying to see the children in these boxes!

Martin himself had a daughter who survived premature birth. He understood what the parents of such children were going through. He wanted to make saving premature babies possible and affordable. There was a problem though, he wasn't a doctor. However, he never allowed that to get in his way.

His dream was realized in 1903 when he opened *two* incubator exhibits. One at Dreamland and the other at

Luna Park, both on Coney Island. He had nurses and doctors attend to the premature babies while strangers would buy tickets to see the sideshow. The cost of caring for a single preemie was about $15 (more than $400 today) a day. All his costs were covered by those who bought the 25-cent tickets. Even his own daughter worked as a nurse, as if to prove that premature babies could grow up to become healthy and strong.

No one ever found out that he was not an educated doctor and continued to send him preemies. Some doctors even attended his attractions themselves to study his methods. In the 50 years that he had his exhibitions, it is estimated that he had received about 8,000 premature babies. He had an 85% success rate, and about 6,500 of these babies got a chance to grow up. Although it's difficult to confirm exact numbers, at the time, he was employing the best nurses and doctors that America had.

He accepted all children, no matter their social background or skin color. He even had a small celebration for babies who had 'graduated' from the incubators on July 25, 1934. Of the 58 babies he had cared for in 1933, 41 came to the reunion and attracted

even more attention to what he had done. Many of his 'graduates' who successfully grew into adults owe their lives to a man that felt the so-called 'weaklings' needed a fighting chance.

Seeing the success Martin had achieved, in 1943, many more hospitals started adopting his incubator idea. This led to more premature children surviving and thriving to become healthy and strong children. With the rate of premature births being 1 in 10, there is a chance that you or someone you know spent some time in an incubator. It is thanks to Martin that this is all possible.

Made in the USA
Coppell, TX
17 September 2022

83296571R00063